a kingdom coming

a kingdom coming

by william c. marrin

an overview of the new testament and its message for us

Nihil Obstat:
    Rev. Hilarion Kistner, O.F.M.
    Rev. Eugene Maly

Imprimi Potest:
    Rev. Andrew Fox, O.F.M.
    Provincial

Imprimatur:
    +Daniel E. Pilarczyk, V.G.
    Archdiocese of Cincinnati
    November 25, 1977

The *Nihil Obstat* and *Imprimatur* are a declaration that a book or pamphlet is considered to be free from doctrinal or moral error. It is not implied that those who have granted the *Nihil Obstat* and *Imprimatur* agree with the contents, opinions or statements expressed.

Illustrations and cover by Kieran Quinn

SBN 0-912228-38-5

Contents

Introduction

Man is an odd creature: an animal with a face, a visionary beast. Frogs seem to have no trouble being frogs; but we humans, tossed up from nature's teeming ocean into the light of self-awareness, look in awe beyond our immediate time, place and instinct and wonder what we are. Our humanity is presented to us not as a given, but as a quest, a project.

But the project has limits. Growing, developing, our being nevertheless balances at every moment upon an animal organism. After six or seven decades—even if by patience and discipline we *have matured to an exquisite sensitivity and wisdom—we must once again fall back into the teeming darkness as surely as any nameless frog.*

How can such a riddle exist? Does it make any sense? Somehow it must. Without meaning we die even while we go on living. But what meaning is there?

This is the realm and question of religion—and throughout history the number and variety of answers have been enormous. The purpose of this short volume is to clarify, in some measure, the unique answer offered by the Bible: Christ and his Kingdom.

For the Bible is not an easy book. True, parts of it are accessible to almost anyone who might pick it up. But a person looking for more than a superficial knowledge must expect page after page of obscure names and places, unfamiliar ritual, archaic ideas and apparent contradictions.

Most of us know people who, with all good intentions, resolved to read the whole thing through from Genesis—and got maybe as far as Leviticus. Sadder but no wiser they settled again for less venturesome sources, like Sunday sermons, convinced that the Bible was not for them.

Others of course are determined that the Bible *will* be for them, that as God's Word it must be taken seriously. But ready to make any necessary sacrifice, they are sometimes led to sacrifice even their intellectual integrity. They fence off the Scriptures from the results of modern archaeology, linguistics and history. If God says that he made the world in six days or that Jonah lived in a big fish's belly, then that's what happened and let's have no more discussion. This position is known as fundamentalism.

But if one is willing to grow and be changed, it's possible to steer a course between these pitfalls in two ways.

The first involves study. We have to learn about a world far different from our own. No one would pick up *Canterbury Tales,* for instance, without some grasp of 14th-century England; and the world of the Bible is four to five times more remote. It's no surprise that someone who ventures into it unguided is soon bewildered.

"Wait," the fundamentalist says. "Biblical statements speak to all men of all times. Their meaning is obvious to anyone who will listen." Sometimes this position is presented as a defense of the truth or inspiration of the Bible. But fundamentalists are scarcely the only ones who believe the Bible is inspired.

The real question is not *"Is* it true?" but *"What* is true? *What* does it actually mean to say?" And the tradition of the Church, going back as far as Jerome, Augustine and Athanasius, is this: The inspired truth of a biblical statement is not the "obvious" thought it brings to mind in this or that reader now, but the religious message intended by the prophet, evangelist or scribe who wrote it in the idioms and thought-patterns of his day.

This principle is highlighted by the fact that our century has unprecedented resources for knowing the past. Scientific techniques for uncovering, classifying and reconstructing the ancient world have become so good that we know

3

the history of Israel, for example, far better than Peter or Paul could. And experts today have more data about Peter and Paul than their own successors did even 50 years later.

Many of our problems with the Bible are resolved when we put this knowledge to work. We find that we had misunderstood the writer's intention: he was telling a parable to teach us a lesson, for example, and we thought it was a news item. By studying the original historical setting, we find out what he meant—and in the process we often get to know a person of great faith.

Which brings us to the second requirement—a willingness to grow in faith. Let me explain it this way: When I was younger I used to wish I had lived in biblical times because it seemed God was so much more active then. It would be easy to believe, I thought, if fire were falling from heaven upon the wicked or seas dividing to let me cross. Nowadays everything seems so ordinary.

But let's take the exodus story. Suppose, instead of walls of water to the left and right with a dry path in between, the Jews were able to cross because a perfectly natural wind came up and blew hard all night, causing a very low tide. Would that mean God was not involved? Would not the love of God have been there in that wind?

If you read Exodus 14:21 you'll see that this is exactly what happened. The other story—that the waters jumped out of the way when the Jews came along—is a celebration in poetic imagery of God's care for his people (Psalm 78:13, for example). If you look again at Exodus 14:21-22, you'll see that the final editor has placed both versions side by

4

side—the plain fact in one verse and the poetry in the other—because the poetry was the best way he had to express his faith: God's hand had saved them.

I don't envy the people of those times anymore. I realize that with faith I too can see God's hand at work in my life—even in the most natural events. I believe that miracles sometimes happen; God seems to have reserved the right to baffle scientists from time to time, just to show them that the most important questions are outside their field. But I also know that we don't have to escape from the human things, the small, ordinary joys and sorrows of every day, to find God. He is in our midst; and our lives, limited as they are, are endowed with meaning beyond all anticipation.

What meaning? Let's look at the Bible.

I Old Testament

No one knows when the first *Adam* (the Hebrew word for *man)* walked the earth. Anthropologists are discovering man-like remains that date back a few million years. Roughly 500,000 years ago lived *homo erectus,* unanimously agreed to be human but still quite primitive. By 50,000 years ago, to judge by skeletons, people were beginning to look much the same as they do today. About 10,000 years ago, these prehistoric men learned to raise plants and animals for themselves instead of foraging around for their food, and this meant they could settle down in permanent homes. Villages became towns, towns united into empires, and civilization developed to the point where, about 5,000 years ago, men learned to write; prehistoric times gave way to recorded history. And the history of Israel begins nearly 2,000 years after that, with the exodus from Egypt at the time of Pharaoh Ramses II.

But why study the history of Israel? Let me offer two reasons, one general and one more specific.

The general reason is that history gives us our identity. The person with amnesia, who can't remember his past, doesn't know who he is. A nation that forgot everything would soon be back living in caves.

The more specific reason is that the story of Israel, insignificant in many ways, is the history that led up to Jesus, the history from which he forged his identity. The Old Testament records a thousand years of struggle and growth, of people gradually learning to know and serve God more adequately—and, we believe, of God active in men's lives, shaping them by his Word and his Spirit, teaching them what to hope for.

A woman who recently read the Old Testament for the first time came to tell me that it disturbed her. Reading it through, she got the impression that God was gradually becoming more mature. In the earlier stories, she said, he appears arbitrary and violent, destroying the whole human race in a flood or commanding the slaughter of entire villages. Later on he grows more reliable, patient, willing to forgive and more reasonable in his requirements.

8

The discovery shook her faith because she had never realized that the Word of God was written by men, with human limitations, in particular historical circumstances. But the shock led to new insight: What happened in the Old Testament period was not, of course, that *God* became more mature but that the *people* who wrote about him did.

Thus monotheism, for example, did not develop overnight. Moses in the 13th century B.C. seems to have presumed that other gods did, in fact, exist when he sang, "Who is like to you among the gods, O Lord?" (Exodus 15:11). The first commandment of the decalogue shows the same way of thinking. Scholars call it *heno*theism: though other gods might exist (see also Judges 11:23-24), the Israelites worship only Yahweh, who brought them out from Egypt and into the promised land. He is their God, they are his people.

Before long this faith progresses to the point that Yahweh is known to be the God who made all things (Genesis 2:4 ff). By the seventh century B.C., the prophets ridicule foreign gods as powerless (e.g., Jeremiah 10: 1-16). And the experience of exile in the sixth century B.C. finally crystallizes a monotheism that is absolute (Isaiah 44:6 ff). The earlier belief in other heavenly beings remains only in the notion of angels.

Appreciation for the dignity of each human life developed in a similar way. Early writings consider the tribe, not the individual, to be the principal object of God's concern. Rewards or punishments for moral behavior are thought to fall upon the whole group, not merely on the responsi-

9

ble individuals (see Joshua 7:1 ff or Exodus 20:5). There is no belief in personal immortality (Psalm 6:5; 88:12; etc.). Only when the nation was destroyed as a political unit by Babylonian armies do we find prophets speaking of a relationship between God and each person individually (Ezekiel 18); and only at the very end of Old Testament times does Israel dare believe that this relationship is stronger than death (e.g., Daniel 12:1-3).

Each deeper insight grew out of experience, sometimes very painful experience, confronted by a faith which trusted that whatever happened, Yahweh somehow stood behind it. And because of this, the developing thought of the Old Testament can be brought together by studying it in the framework of the historical events which provoked it. Let me offer a brief outline of those events:

13th to 11th Centuries B.C.:
Exodus and the Occupation of the Promised Land

For no apparent merit on their part, a group of Semitic slaves in Egypt is set free by the power of a God who has revealed himself to Moses. This God binds them to himself by a covenant and leads them through the Sinai desert with the promise of "a land of milk and honey." This is the beginning of Israel's history as a nation. The stories of earlier times in the book of Genesis are actually prehistoric, that is, they represent memories handed down orally for centuries before the Sinai Covenant, before Yahweh was worshipped, before Israel in the true sense came to exist. While there are historical recollections contained in them, they have been shaped by constant retelling to reflect the faith of a later time. Compare, for example, the use of the name *Yahweh* in the story of Abraham and Isaac (Genesis 22) with the more accurate statement in Exodus 6:3.

This period is one of continual conflict. As a result, Yahweh is understood primarily as "God of Hosts"—that is, God of Armies, who smites first Egypt, then the Canaanites, then the Philistines with his "strong right arm." Read Judges 5 for a poem that captures the spirit of these times.

10th Century B.C.:
The Glorious Kingdom

David is anointed king, "messiah," in 1012 B.C. and he pushes back the Philistine armies that have plagued the Israelites for almost two centuries. The land of milk and honey is finally theirs. In the joy of triumph, David is celebrated as God's "Son," or representative, with title to rule the whole world (Psalms 2 and 110). The splendor achieved by David's son Solomon almost seems to justify such extravagant talk.

With peace and prosperity comes reflection on God's glory in creation and, above all, in man. Psalm 8 expresses the optimism and confidence of these idyllic times.

9th to 7th Centuries B.C.:
The Honeymoon Is Over

At the end of Solomon's reign, the northern half of his kingdom breaks away in civil war. This is followed by an endless series of military and economic disasters. The people are inclined to quit Yahweh and find a more successful deity. Against this, the prophets announce that their troubles are due to their sins (e.g., Isaiah 1:19-20). They must turn back to just ways. Some prophets speak in terms of a holy and righteous messiah who will see that God's will is carried out (Isaiah 9:6-7; 11:1-5). Then the paradisal Kingdom God promised will finally come about.

6th Century B.C.:
Exile

The northern tribes had fallen to Assyria in 722, and now in 587, Babylonian armies overwhelmed the Davidic kingdom in the south, carrying the people off to captivity in Mesopotamia. Besides the misery of defeat itself, the event had a devasting effect on their faith, for the prophets had assured them that David's throne would stand forever (e.g., Isaiah 37:35). Was Yahweh powerless? Or had their sins been so great as to exhaust his patience? Either way, Israel's existence seemed ended, its people scattered in a foreign land.

But in this greatest of crises, the prophets reached their profoundest insight: God remains loyal and loving, beyond all anticipation. The people had indeed broken the covenant by sin, but he would take them back, make a new covenant with them (Jeremiah 31:31), and put his own Spirit in their hearts (Ezekiel 36:27). The dead bones of Israel would live again (Ezekiel 37). No matter how great man's sin, God's forgiveness is greater.

5th Century Onward: Frustration

Cyrus the Persian decreed in 538 B.C. that the Jews could return home, and by 500 many had done so. Encouraged by the prophets (e.g., Isaiah 49—not from Isaiah himself but from an unknown prophet of the exile), they thought they would finally possess the messianic Kingdom they were made for.

They were sorely disappointed. They found themselves in an impoverished land with no king of their own, heavily taxed by their foreign over-lords. By the fourth century there was no longer even a prophet to interpret the times.

God seemed absent, the heavens sealed over. Why did he not act? How long, O Lord? The mood of the last centuries before Christ was one of suspense.

CHAPTER ONE: OLD TESTAMENT

Further Readings
1) **Exodus 19** — The Mosaic Covenant, the foundation of Old Testament religion. In effect, Yahweh says to Israel, "I will be your God," and Israel agrees, "We will be your people."
2) **Isaiah 40** — Chapters 40-55 of the book of Isaiah were written by an unknown prophet of the exile. Israel has repeatedly rejected

Yahweh and deserves to be cast away. But Yahweh's love knows no measure: "Can a mother forget her infant, be without tenderness for the child of her womb? Even should she forget, I will never forget you" (Isaiah 49:15).

Discussion Starters
1) "The Old Testament records . . . God active in men's lives, shaping them by his Word and Spirit, teaching them what to hope for." What are the things that *you* hope for in day-to-day living? Is it realistic to think that your hopes might be shaped by God's Word? What does God ask us to hope for?
2) Is there a parallel between the way the writers of the Scriptures gradually became aware of who God is and the way we ourselves become aware of the same reality? What has shaped your ideas about God thus far in your life? Do you think these ideas will need further revision?
3) "No matter how great man's sin, God's forgiveness is greater." What does it take to become convinced of this?
4) What can we learn from our own periodic experiences of the "absence of God"?

II The Torah and the Pharisees

We all know who the Pharisees were — the bad guys. But if we lived in Palestine in the years before Christ, we would have a different opinion.

They were painful times. Except for a few generations of independence won by the Maccabees, the Jews had served one foreign government after another for the five centuries since their return from exile: first Persians, then Greeks, and now the Romans. There were economic restrictions and heavy taxes, infringements on religious freedom and, at times, even persecution—probably not unlike Ireland under British rule, for example. And the Pharisees' way of coping with all this was not too bad. Consider the gamut of options:

There were *Sadducees.* Hereditary priest-aristocrats, they maintained their position of wealth and power through control of worship at the Temple, on the one hand, and through shrewd cooperation with foreign overlords, on the other. Although they held the highest religious offices, they were scarcely noted for piety. Their best interests were served by paying lip-service to the ancient religious traditions that put them in power while being totally secular in their day-to-day decisions. Caiaphas, the high priest who schemed the death of Jesus, was a Sadducee (Matthew 26:3).

There were *Essenes*—not mentioned in the Bible but important for New Testament background. They were a radical sect so disturbed by Sadducee control of the Temple priesthood in Jerusalem that they set up communes in the desert—most notably at Qumran, by the shores of the Dead Sea. Writings from their library, the "Dead Sea Scrolls," have been discovered there in recent years. They lived lives of highly organized and rigorous obedience to God, and waited for him to destroy the corruption they saw everywhere else.

There were *Zealots.* These hot-headed rebels thought that anything would be better than the present powerlessness. They believed that God's promises to Israel could be fulfilled by a violent overthrow of the foreign regime; their assassinations and guerrilla uprisings had a religious fanaticism to them. Zealot leaders would sometimes, in fact, claim the title *messiah.* But the New Testament calls them "bandits." Barabbas was probably one of them, "a man who had committed murder in an insurrection" (Mark 15:7). The Zealot position finally prevailed, leading the Jews into a disastrous rebellion that ended with the destruction of Jerusalem by Roman armies in 70 A.D.

There were also *emigrants,* like the prodigal son in the parable, who left the poverty of Palestine to seek their fortunes in Damascus, Antioch or Alexandria. Nearly every sizeable city between Babylon and Rome had its colony of expatriate Jews.

There were the *poor working people,* too preoccupied with daily survival to take much interest in religious observances.

And, finally, there were the *Pharisees.* They appear in the New Testament as living in a tangle of odd regulations about what is permitted on the Sabbath, how many times a day to pray, or how to wash your hands and dishes. But the rules have a positive side, too. The fact that they reach into every aspect of life is proof of the Pharisees' genuine and pious desire to obey God's will in all things (see Psalm 119). They took their religion seriously.

While the Torah (meaning Law or Instruction, the revealed will of God) had been part of Israel's religion from the start, it had not always been the all-embracing center of devotion. This new emphasis developed as a way of relating to God in the time of Babylonian exile, when the Temple was destroyed. It expanded still more in the frustration that followed the homecoming.

For the Jews had returned to Palestine full of hope. They felt forgiven, graced, restored; prophets said that all God's promises were about to be fulfilled. But nothing happened. And then there were no more prophets. Was God with them or not? Unable to see his hand at work around them, they turned more and more to the security of the past. The sacred books were codified and studied; the regulations were enforced more rigorously.

Ezra the scribe (about 400 B.C.—see Nehemiah 8) is especially remembered as the great promulgator of the Torah. Over the years other great teachers and scholars ("scribes") offered still further instructions, spelling out God's will in greater detail to bridge the gap between the original legislation of the Pentateuch, now centuries old, and the daily lives of the devout. Meeting every week in synagogues, pious Jews immersed themselves as thoroughly as possible in knowledge of both the written Scriptures and the traditions of the great scribes. Obedience to God's will was the sum and substance of their religion.

This devotion to the Law gave them an impressive strength, a sense of identity that weathered all storms. After the tragic war that destroyed Jerusalem, it was the Pharisees more than anyone else who preserved Jewish faith for future generations. But their strength was also their weakness. The strong walls of tradition which sustained them tended to become a prison, trapping them in a smug and inflexible stance. They were so scrupulously searching for God's will in the past, they could not see it when it stood

20

before them in the present.

Their religious approach suffered from externalism — the substitution of outward performance for interior motivation. Our Catholic experience with fish-on-Friday could offer a parallel to their absorption with the letter of the law. I know people who could have told you, say, whether turtle soup counted as meat or fish, but never thought of the inner sense of penance that the law was designed for.

Along with this went a legalistic view of life, in which every possible situation was described by rules. Every rule has exceptions, but the legalist can't bear the responsibility for making them. He wants a rule for the exception, too. The result is a legal prison cut off from life, like a country with a constitution that can't be amended.

And underlying these things was a false image of God. They imagined God as distant, as a fair employer who rewards service justly. They wanted to be safe with him, to know where they stood with no surprises. They were shocked at Jesus' ideas of a God who delights in forgiving sinners (in Luke 15, for example).

But we should remember that they were good people, upright, religious, dedicated. Jesus excoriated them the way you can only fight with someone very close to you, because he loved them dearly.

CHAPTER TWO, THE TORAH AND THE PHARISEES

Further Readings
1) **Matthew 5-7** — The Sermon on the Mount. The new law which Jesus gives is the fulfillment of the Mosaic Torah given on Mt. Sinai.
2) **John 15** (especially verses 8-17) — See also the words of Paul: "The whole law has found its fulfillment in this one saying: 'You shall love your neighbor as yourself.' " (Galatians 5:14). Perhaps John's version is more demanding, telling us to love not merely as *we* love ourselves but as *Jesus* loves us.

Discussion Starters
1) The Zealots were religious fanatics. What qualifies a person or group to be called fanatic? Can it be wrong to be fanatic in the service of religion?
2) "Obedience to God's will was the sum and substance of their [pious Jews'] religion." What is the sum and substance of *our* religion?
3) "They were so scrupulously searching for God's will in the past, they could not see it when it stood before them in the present." How can we hope to discover God's will for *us* at any given moment? Does he still speak in our own times?
4) Is it possible even today that devotion to law can entrap people in a "smug and inflexible

stance"? What is the Christian attitude toward law?

5) Is God a "fair employer who rewards service justly"? After giving your spontaneous answer, read Matthew 20:1-16. Does it cause you to revise your image of God?

III Apocalypse

When Jesus went about announcing "The reign of God is at hand" (Mark 1:15), he got instant attention. No one but the complacent Sadducees could hear those words without getting excited.

The expression translated into English as "the Reign of God" or "the Kingdom of God" sums up a thousand years of Jewish hopes. Starting with the ancient dream of "a land flowing with milk and honey" and reshaped by countless prophets and teachers, it had come to represent the goal of all history, the reason for man's existence. But it had also become enmeshed in a new way of looking at the world, a new religious atmosphere known as *apocalyptic.*

To appreciate this development more fully, let's look again at Israel's experience after the Babylonian exile.

In the previous chapter, I described the Pharisees' approach to God. One way to explain their excess is that they listened too well to the ancient prophets. In the years before the exile, the prophets had called Israel to repentance with the explanation that the sufferings they experienced were due to sin. The prophets went mostly unheard at first, but after the terrible experience of exile, the Jews tried to prevent further disasters by purifying the people of all sin. The Pharisaic approach to law is the end product of this anxiety.

By the same token, the prophets had also promised that obedience to God would bring blessings, and these blessings came to be summed up under the heading of the Kingdom, or Reign, of God. We tend to presume, mistakenly, that this meant "heaven," a place of salvation for souls after death. But Judaism didn't think in terms of souls, in our sense. The Reign of God referred to a future Israel in this world, enjoying all the good things described by the prophets: swords beaten into ploughshares, lion and lamb at peace, the outpouring of the Holy Spirit on all flesh, an end to tears and sin, God ruling through a chosen king ("messiah").

The prophets' descriptions of the Kingdom make no mention of a salvation for those already dead—it was to be for the living. The doctrine of the resurrection of the dead developed only about the third century B.C., and of all Old Testament books only Daniel and II Maccabees refer to it. The conservative Sadducees never did accept the idea.

When this belief in resurrection finally broke into Jewish thought, it was part of a new wave of religious imagery which owes something to the influence of Persia. The Persians (who ruled Israel for two centuries after the exile) explained the existence of evil in the world not primarily in terms of human sinfulness, but as the effect of evil spirits. Their faith was that these forces of darkness, which dominated the world at present, would one day be defeated by the armies of light. Then mankind would rise from the dead to be judged by fire; those who proved righteous would enjoy eternal life.

Jewish tradition was too convinced of human responsibility, and too wedded to the reality of this world, to accept these ideas easily. But as years went on, as times became worse instead of better, as the hopes raised by the prophets remained unfulfilled, and as the sense of God's absence grew stronger, the idea that the present order of the world is indeed dominated by evil forces grew more convincing. Jews began to see the coming of God's Reign less and less in terms of their own conversion and more as God's mighty intervention. When the predestined moment arrived, they imagined him unleashing his wrath upon all evildoers in a cosmic holocaust and introducing an entirely new age in which creation would be the paradise intended from the beginning.

This new apocalyptic mentality finds its first full-fledged literary expression in the Book of Daniel. The Jews had grown used to harassment by foreign overlords, but in 168 B.C. the Syrian King Antiochus IV went beyond all limits. To consolidate his strength against the expanding power of the Romans, he violated the Temple of Jerusalem, robbed its ornaments and treasures, set up a pagan altar in the sanctuary and demanded that the Jews worship *him* as a manifestation of Zeus. It was beyond endurance. The Jews were willing to die instead.

And they did. Read II Maccabees 6:18—7:42 to see what torments they suffered for their faith. This must be the end, people thought. God must put a stop to this. They pored over the prophets' writings for clues, trying to wring from them some sign of how long the present evil age would go on before God's Reign would come. And an unknown scribe composed the Book of Daniel to reassure a tortured people that it would be soon.

From then on through the time of Christ, the apocalyptic mood was never far below the surface of Palestinian Judaism. There was a pervasive sense that the world was collapsing, that anything might happen, that history was coming to an explosive climax. The Jews begged God for that climax; only then would the world be freed from its servitude to evil and all things be made new. "Thy Kingdom come" was not a new prayer invented by Jesus.

We're familiar with only the two apocalyptic books that were included in the Bible: Daniel in the Old Testament and the Book of Revelation in the New. But many other apocalypses circulated in those days. Each was attributed to some famous figure of Jewish tradition—Moses, Enoch, Baruch, Ezra, and so on. And all had the same purpose: to encourage endurance in a time of stress. God's people had not been abandoned; their struggle was part of the great, final conflict between good and evil, and it meant that this present evil age would soon be over. The basic message was usually expanded to include timetables of God's "game-plan," arrays of angels preparing to do battle, and the terrible punishments in store for God's enemies. Flamboyant and bizarre imagery overloaded the reader's imagination to create a sense of God's transcendent power.

People looking through the apocalyptic writings today should be careful not to forget this historical background. Fundamentalists of our own times, as of many other times in the past, have gotten caught up in the apocalyptic spirit and thought they saw secret messages and signs, hidden in the text for centuries, only now coming true in our time. What they don't realize is that the apocalyptic writers, with all their mysterious language, were speaking of the events of their own day. The "Abomination of Desolation" (Daniel 12:11), for example, was the pagan altar erected by Antiochus in the sanctuary in Jerusalem. "The harlot that sits on seven hills" (Revelation 17:9) was the city of Rome. And "the beast" (Revelation 13:18) was the emperor Nero. Applications to the present time have to begin from the original meaning intended by the writers.

Obviously the writers' expectations of a

speedy end did not come true, at least not in the way that was envisioned. The power of evil continued to work in the world; the lion and the lamb did not learn to rest together in peace; the new creation remained in the future. But on the other hand, a dramatic, definitive intervention of God into human history was about to take place.

CHAPTER THREE, APOCALYPSE

Further Readings
1) **Daniel 7** — The promise of the Kingdom. The symbolic narrative describes Israel's painful history after the Babylonian exile, culminating in the persecutions of Antiochus IV (verse 25— see also I Maccabees 1). The tyrant will meet "absolute destruction," however, and the whole world will be brought under God's Reign.
2) **Revelation 21** — The promise of God's Reign still stands, purified by the message of Jesus: God will make all things new and dwell in our midst forever.

Discussion Starters
1) How much of the apocalyptic symbolism is to be taken literally?
2) In the face of our experience, is it reasonable to hope that evil will one day be conquered and all things be made new?
3) "They began to see the coming of God's Reign less and less in terms of their own

conversion and more as God's mighty intervention." To what extent does responsibility for changing the world rest in man's own hands?

4) The "end of the world" was an event for which the early Christians prayed fervently. Why is it that thoughts of the same event are so unpleasant for most Christians today?

IV Jesus' Message

"Jesus appeared in Galilee proclaiming the good news of God: 'This is the time of fulfillment. The reign of God is at hand. Reform your lives and believe in the gospel.' "(Mark 1:15).

It should be clear by now that the coming of God's Reign was the good news or "gospel" that Palestine awaited. But why did Jesus ask for reform? The word in the Greek text is *metanoeite*, meaning literally "let your consciousness be transformed." Why would such a change be necessary—wasn't the Kingdom of God exactly what everyone was praying for?

Yes, but what they meant by the Kingdom wasn't what Jesus meant. The Kingdom they expected was imagined along the legalistic and apocalyptic lines described in the previous chapters. What Jesus was announcing was much greater.

First, as regards the Law: The Pharisaic mentality suffered from externalism, legalism and a distorted idea of God.

Externalism receives scathing words—"Woe to you scribes and Pharisees, you frauds! You cleanse the outside of cup and dish and leave the inside filled with loot and lust! ... You are like whitewashed tombs, beautiful to look at on the outside but inside full of filth and dead men's bones" (Matthew 23). But this type of attack was not unique to Jesus; Israel's prophets had a long tradition of similar words for those whose religion was merely external performance (e.g., Amos 5 or Isaiah 58).

Legalism was a more subtle issue because it involved good, pious people. But it was just as serious. Looking for a refuge from ambiguity in an age when so much was going wrong, people had reduced God's will to a set of rules that was sometimes cumbersome but not really challenging. It took no greatness of spirit, for example, to avoid the 39 forbidden activities on the Sabbath. Decent people were able to say, honestly, "All these commandments I have kept since my youth"—and this became the basis for their security and self-satisfaction: "I give you thanks, O God, that I am not like the rest of men" (Luke 18:11).

Such people were good, but they were missing so much. By settling into a snug structure of rules, they were cutting themselves off from life. Commandments and rules are good and necessary; they offer much-needed guidance as we learn to be what we should be. But they go only so far. Laws cannot protect us from wasting our lives in the wrong vocation, for example, or from marrying the wrong wife, or from missing an opportunity to grow in love.

To wake them up, Jesus frequently compared the upright with those who had led disreputable lives, and told the upright they were second-best. "Tax agents and prostitutes are entering the Kingdom of God before you" (Matthew 21:31). The story of the Pharisee and the publican (Luke 18:9-14), the saying about 99 just men and one sinner (Luke 15:7) and the parable of the prodigal son—all make the same point. Jesus wasn't praising sinners for their sin, but he was praising their willingness to change.

"But why should *we* change?" asked the upright. "Because your goodness doesn't go far enough." Jesus sharpened up the demands of the Law: "You have heard the commandment imposed on your forefathers, 'You shall not commit murder. . . .' What I say to you is everyone who grows angry with his brother shall be liable to judgment. . . . You have heard the commandment, 'You shall love your countryman but hate your enemy.' My command to you is: love your enemies, pray for your persecutors" (Matthew 5:20-48). The demands that he makes go beyond all measure—men are told to forgive without counting the cost, to lend without expecting repayment, to turn the other cheek, to "be perfect, even as your heavenly Father is perfect."

There is no room left for self-satisfaction in anyone who really hears Jesus' words.

And having cut away the security they found in their legalism, Jesus offers a whole new vision of God.

The Pharisees had made God a taskmaster, measuring out rewards according to their obedience. But by insisting on the security of a contract-like arrangement, they were blind to the abundant life he wanted to share with them as his beloved children (Luke 17:5-10). God is like the recklessly generous landowner giving rewards even to those who have worked a short time (Matthew 20:1-16), the father embracing the son who squandered half his possessions (Luke 15:11-32). Open your heart, discover how great is his love for you, begin to live as his son or daughter; set out on the unique adventure your life was meant to be (Matthew 6:30-33).

The other problem in understanding what Jesus meant by the Kingdom centered upon apocalyptic speculation. Feeling like an embattled minority in a corrupt world, desperate for some relief, people were trying to calculate the time when God's Reign would come. Watching for signs in the stars or combing the Scriptures for clues, they ached for the day when their enemies would be destroyed by fire from heaven; when the pious, Law-keeping Jews would be vindicated; when all things would finally be as they were meant to be. The Zealots thought they could hurry things along by fighting the pagans themselves.

The Kingdom of God doesn't come that way, Jesus told them. And you can't calculate its arrival. By focusing your attention on the future you are avoiding your responsibility in the present. The future will come, but at a time when you least expect it (Matthew 24:44). Only the Father knows the day (Mark 13:32).

But in a real way it is also close to you, even now as I speak to you (Luke 4:21). Its rich new life is at your fingertips, if you will only open your hearts to it (Luke 17:21). You look for signs in the sky but you are blind to the signs before you (see Luke 7:22).

You expect a Kingdom you can enter without being transformed, a Kingdom that you have already earned, or that you could bring about by seizing power and making others conform to your measure. But the Reign of God is something better, something you have scarcely begun to imagine. You can taste it though, now, if you will open your heart to my words.

Begin to love as the Father loves. Begin to forgive as he forgives, to live generously without counting the cost; be willing even to surrender your life if necessary. The new life you long for is possible now, if you believe.

CHAPTER FOUR, JESUS' MESSAGE

Further Readings

1) **Luke 6** — Verses 17 to 49 give St. Luke's version of what we know more familiarly as Matthew's "Sermon on the Mount." It can help

us get a fresh look at what Jesus was saying.

2) **Luke 15** — We begin to be part of God's Kingdom to the extent that we know and imitate him. Here are three parables in which Jesus spells out God's true nature.

Discussion Starters

1) How does someone who has heard Jesus' call for reform look at the world? What changes when our "consciousness is transformed"?
2) What criteria can be used to judge our religious practices, to determine whether they are mere externalism or true signs of God's Reign dawning in our lives?
3) Does the way of life to which Jesus invites us seem beyond the reach of ordinary people? Is it realistic to think we can shape our lives around his teachings? Can a believer survive in this world?
4) Reread the last paragraph of this chapter. Do you believe it?

V Birth of the Church

For a number of years after Jesus' death and resurrection, the apostles had no intention of founding a new Church. The Church to them was Israel, the chosen people of God.

Christianity and Judaism, as we know them today, are separated by centuries of hostility, and it's hard to imagine anything different. But at the beginning, Jesus' followers still considered themselves Jews. They observed the Torah and the Jewish holy days; they offered sacrifice in the Temple in Jerusalem; and they studied the Scriptures (the part we call the Old Testament, of course—there was no New Testament yet) in the synagogues.

What was different about them was their mission. They believed that God had called them to carry on Jesus' own work of announcing the Kingdom of God. Through them, God was preparing the hearts of his people for the new age that was drawing near. The 12 apostles symbolized the beginnings of a renewed and holy 12 tribes of Israel.

Their proclamation to their countrymen was much the same as Jesus' had been, though his crucifixion, of course, had added weight to its challenge and the resurrection stood as a divine testimony to its urgency: "Be converted and believe the good news." Many of those who did believe the message sold their property, gave the proceeds to a common fund, and started preparing themselves for the end of the age. Others hurried to spread the word; they believed they would not even get through all the towns of Israel before the end (see Matthew 10:23).

And they met considerable success. Read Acts 2:44-47, for example, for St. Luke's report. Remember that they were not asking Jews to give up being Jewish; they were not making converts to a new religion but to a new "Way" (Acts 9:2), to a movement of renewal within Judaism. Their only major enemies were the Sadducee high priests who had plotted against Jesus (Acts 4:11 and 5:17). The attitude of pious Pharisees was more like that of the Rabbi Gamaliel: "If their purpose or activity is human in its origins, it will destroy itself. If, on the other hand, it comes from God, you will not be able to destroy them without fighting God himself" (Acts 5:38-39).

But trouble was coming. Jesus in effect had placed himself above Moses, reinterpreting Moses' teachings and claiming an unprecedented, even absolute, authority. So long as his disciples continued to observe the Torah, this would cause no great dissension. But what if occasion arose to call the Law of Moses into question?

Some were faced with this challenge more quickly than others. The insight occurred first among converts from the more cosmopolitan, Greek-speaking group of Jews known as "Hellenists"; perhaps their education led them to think instinctively of the wider world. When one of their leaders, named Stephen, proclaimed eloquently that Jesus "will change the customs which Moses handed down to us" (Acts 6:14), the Pharisees, who had previously remained neutral, became incensed. Stephen was stoned to death, the first Christian martyr. Persecution broke out, and the Hellenists fled. Saul, a zealous young Pharisee, was one of those who went out with warrants to arrest them.

But not all Jesus' disciples were persecuted; only those who were "subverting the Law of Moses." In the midst of it all, the apostles in Jerusalem were untouched (Acts 8:1). For they had not agreed with Stephen; to them the Torah was still sacred. They quoted Jesus' saying that not one iota of the Law would pass away until the consummation of the world (Matthew 5:18). Eventually it took a special act of God (the vision described in Acts 10) to convince St. Peter that his ancestral customs were not as inviolable as he thought.

Meanwhile the Hellenists had scattered to foreign lands and had begun baptizing Gentiles into their fellowship (Acts 11:20). The disciples in Jerusalem were appalled. The converts must first be circumcised, they said. Otherwise any Jew who associated with them (and above all, who broke bread with them) would be rendered unclean.

Even when St. Peter was convinced by his vision that Jewish Christians were not to worry about this law themselves, the dilemma remained: other Jews would shun them if they fraternized with Gentiles. How could they carry on Jesus' mission in Palestine if they allowed the uncircumcised into their community?

Peter's greatness as the rock of Church unity begins to emerge in this difficult period. Somehow he managed to keep together two opposing parties: one which brought in converts without regard for Jewish tradition, and the other which insisted that Christ's mission was only to the "lost sheep of the House of Israel" (Matthew 15:24). Peter finally had to flee Jerusalem himself in 43 A.D., leaving the mother Church in the care of the very cautious, Torah-keeping James. He was back again in 49 for the Church's first council, mediating between James and Paul (Acts 15), but his work was now elsewhere.

The center of the new community was moving away from Jerusalem. Jesus' "Way" was much more than just a call to reform Israel. The writings of Saul the Pharisee, who had now become Paul the Apostle to the Gentiles, show a man struggling with the consequences of this realization. He shared in St. Peter's effort to keep Jewish and Gentile converts from excommunicating each other (though he sometimes disagreed with Peter's methods; see Galatians 2:11). He understood the new community drawn from both Jews and Greeks to be in fact a new Chosen People, heirs of God's promises to Abraham. He continued to go first to the synagogue in every city where he preached the gospel, but those Jews who would not listen were renouncing their claim to membership in the People of God.

And slowly the number of Greek converts grew until they outnumbered the Christians of Jewish origin. There was still a community of Christians in Palestine carefully observing the Jewish Law and hoping to convert their fellow Jews to Christ. But in the years 60-65 A.D., when Zealot opinion prevailed and Palestine began organizing for a war of independence against Rome, the Christians could not cooperate. They knew that God's Kingdom was not to be achieved by warfare. When the armies gather, "Those in Judea at the time must flee to the mountains," says Luke 21:21, and they did. Torah-keeping Christians were scattered, Jerusalem was demolished by Roman armies in 70 A.D., and Jewish Christianity slowly disappeared from history.

Meanwhile a remarkable achievement was taking place in the wider, Greek-speaking Mediterranean world. Let me put it this way: The proclamation of Jesus in Palestine was endlessly profound and challenging, but not intricate or complex. It is not impossible to present his message in a few short parables, as he often did, or to summarize it in a short chapter. But the Church as we know it is far from simple in its rules, doctrines, rituals and organization. How did the change come about?

First, when Jesus spoke, he was addressing a people whom God had been preparing for almost 1,300 years. There was a context for his words, a vocabulary he could use, a tradition he could speak to. But when his disciples went out to the Greek world, they had no such context. Not even the word *God* had the same meaning. There were different traditions of prayer, of worship, of morality, of community life—in short, the message of Jesus had to be translated into an entire new way of living.

Along with this came the realization that their mission was much more vast than they had anticipated. At first, the apostolic generation had believed that history was almost at an end. Jesus was expected to come back very soon "to judge the living and the dead." Even in the 50's St. Paul wrote as if he expected to be still one of the living when Jesus returned (I Thessalonians 4:15). And people in that frame of mind don't write books for posterity or establish codes of canon law. But gradually it was realized that there might be an indefinite period yet to come before all things were accomplished.

These two factors together put a tremendous challenge to the new community — that it become an organized Church. Guided by the Risen Lord and his Holy Spirit in their midst, this is precisely what the first-century Christians accomplished.

CHAPTER FIVE, THE BIRTH OF THE CHURCH

Further Readings

1) **Acts 10** — The story of Peter's realization that the new life he has found in Jesus is to be proclaimed to all men, not just to Jews.
2) **I Thessalonians 5** — Paul's letter conveys the excitement of a Church which expected the return of Christ at any time.
3) **Romans 11** — Paul says that the Jews are still God's chosen people. If we are favored, it is as wild branches grafted onto the natural olive tree.

Discussion Starters

1) "Christianity and Judaism as we know them today are separated by centuries of hostility, and it's hard to imagine anything different." Have you encountered anti-Semitism among Christians? If the roots of Christianity are in Judaism, why are there such deep differences between the two?
2) Christianity took shape slowly over a period of time. Could it be that its shape is still changing? How does that prospect make you feel? In what way would you say that the Church must be complete as it is? In what way is it still developing?
3) By the end of the New Testament period, the

Church seemed to have exchanged its earlier air of excitement for a more settled and orderly existence. What was the reason for this? Was it a positive development or a negative one, and why?

4) Does a better knowledge of the first-century Church reassure you about the changes we have experienced since Vatican II?

VI Paul

The epistles of St. Paul are the earliest Christian writings in existence. Written through the 50's and early 60's, they provide a unique opportunity to see the young Church's life close up. Except for Romans, which Paul wrote to introduce his thinking to a community that didn't yet know him, the letters are unsystematic, specific, totally engaged in the particular needs and concrete issues of the local churches he was addressing—questions of discipline, of encouragement and clarification, even the practical details of collecting money for the poor.

51

The man whose personality emerges from these writings is strong, passionate and intelligent. His presence is so powerful, in fact, that some historians have suggested that he, instead of Jesus, should be counted the real founder of Christian faith.

In their favor, it must be granted that Christianity did not emerge as a religion in its own right, distinct from Judaism, for some years after Jesus' resurrection. As we saw in the previous chapter, the disciples at first confined their ministry to the "lost sheep of the house of Israel," the way Jesus himself had done (e.g., Matthew 15:24).

The missionary insight didn't begin with Paul, however. Its origins go back to the Jewish-Christian Hellenists whom Paul was persecuting at the time of his conversion. These were the first to understand that Jesus' gospel had broken the confines of the Torah, and this was precisely what provoked the outrage of zealous Pharisees like Saul of Tarsus.

Saul was probably a rabbinical student in Jerusalem when St. Stephen was stoned to death (Acts 7:58; see also 22:3 and Philippians 3:6). Only a bystander at first, he became an active persecutor of missionary Christianity as it began to spread (Acts 9:1). But then he met Jesus, risen from the dead; his passion and talent were turned to promoting the very cause he had been fighting.

This new commitment entailed a struggle on two fronts at once. Not only was there the missionary task itself with its exhausting demands (which Paul is quite ready to talk about—see II Corinthians 11:23-29, for example), but there was opposition from some Christian quarters as well. Jesus' followers as a whole were still far from a clear break with Judaism. Especially in Palestine, many continued to observe the Torah carefully, and they wanted Greek converts to do the same.

From our viewpoint centuries later, we find it hard to believe that the Church would ever have had much of a problem distinguishing itself from Judaism. But, in fact, that was the greatest single crisis the fledgling Church had to face. The question was supposedly resolved in the Jerusalem Council of 49 A.D., but five years later Paul's converts in Galatia, for example, were still being harassed by "Judaizers" who told them they couldn't be saved unless they were circumcised.

Besides natural loyalty to their tradition and the early practice of the disciples, the pro-circumcision "Judaizers" could appeal to a theological principle to defend their position: The Law of Moses was given by God himself and was intended to stand until the end of time. Even Jesus had said that "Not the smallest letter of the Law" should be done away with until all things are fulfilled (Matthew 5:18).

The missionary response, as it came to be articulated by St. Paul, contained an astonishing and radical counter-principle: Granted that the Torah was intended to last until Kingdom come, its role is now nonetheless ended because the Kingdom *has* come. All things *have* been accomplished.

Left unqualified, such a claim would easily be refuted by experience—surely this world of confusion and suffering is not the New Creation that

God has been planning for those who love him. (Remember that "Kingdom of God" meant not just a private, spiritual salvation for the soul but resurrection of the body as well, and life everlasting in a transformed creation where God's will is done on earth as it is in heaven.)

But as St. Paul was to explain it, experience was on his side. For although the rest of the world still "groans as if in labor" (Romans 8:22) for a day of salvation yet to come, that day has already been reached by one man, Jesus. In Jesus, the will of God was perfectly fulfilled, even unto death. And in Jesus, the life of the world to come has already begun. Rising from the dead, Jesus has entered upon a dazzling fullness of life which we can scarcely imagine—but which we too were made to share.

And those who join themselves to Jesus can already taste the Kingdom yet to come. If we are willing to "die" with him, trusting the Father enough to give ourselves away in love, then we also "rise" with him and begin to live out even now the God-like life of glory that lies ahead. We share his Holy Spirit, which becomes the principle of our lives as it was of his. And in a real sense we share his very self, his risen existence. We become his risen Body.

This may suggest a richer view of the Risen Christ than the one we are used to. But we make resurrection too ordinary when we imagine that Jesus simply got back up on his feet on Easter and soared off to heaven 40 days later.

Risen life is a mode of existence beyond anything we can yet comprehend—one which is described sometimes as "enthroned at God's right hand" and sometimes as in the midst of believers "wherever two or three are gathered together." Yet to be a Christian, by Paul's definition, is to begin by faith to experience this new existence. "To live is Christ," he says (Philippians 1:21). "I live now, no longer I, but Christ living in me" (Galatians 2:20). "If anyone is in Christ, he is a new creation" (II Corinthians 5:17).

Paul was essentially a man of action, a born leader, a relentless apostle whose practical contribution to the formation of Christianity can scarcely be estimated. But at the center of his life and work was his experience of the Risen Christ.

CHAPTER SIX, PAUL

Further Readings

1) **I Corinthians 15** — Paul's preaching on the centrality of the resurrection for Christian life.
2) **II Corinthians 10, 11, 12** — A long passage but worth the effort for the view it gives of Paul's passionate personality.
3) **Colossians 3:1-17** — How do Christians share in the risen life of Christ? St. Paul here answers the question.

Discussion Starters

1) Jesus tells us that he has no use for lukewarm people, that we should be either hot or cold. Paul, obviously, was not lukewarm. Is it necessary for us to be as passionate about our

faith as Paul was about his?

2) The role of the Mosaic Law is ended because the Kingdom of God has come. What are the implications of this claim? Are the commandments now passe? What pattern of life is a Christian to follow?

3) Discuss the concept of the resurrection presented in this chapter. What new insights did it hold for you? How does it compare with what you previously thought about resurrection?

VII Matthew, Mark, Luke

What strikes you most about Matthew, Mark and Luke is probably *not* their originality. At least two-thirds of their total content is repeated nearly word for word either by two or by all three of them. For this reason they are often called the *Synoptic* Gospels, from the Greek word meaning "a common view." But then you aren't looking for originality when you pick up these writings. You want the words and deeds of Jesus, and you want them presented as faithfully as possible.

Still, there are three different authors here, writing in three different times and circumstances.

Most people have never read even one of the Gospels all the way through—let alone all three—and have never compared one with another where the material overlaps. When you do, though, you begin to discover three unique personalities.

Mark

St. Mark was probably the John-Mark who appears in the epistles and in Acts. (Jews of the Hellenistic world often used a Greek name like Mark in addition to their Jewish name; Saul-Paul is the best-known example.) If this is the case, he grew up in Jerusalem and enjoyed a somewhat stormy relationship with Paul (Acts 15:37, but also Philemon 24). Tradition makes him a close collaborator of Peter as well (see I Peter 5:13).

His Gospel is sometimes dismissed as a sort of *Reader's Digest* condensation of Matthew, but the overwhelming weight of evidence indicates the opposite—that Mark wrote first (probably in the 60's), and then Matthew used Mark's work, filling it out with additional material. Mark wrote in a Greek that is stylistically primitive, but his achievement was immense. He invented the literary form that we call a gospel.

This requires some explanation. Like the wheel, every great invention seems obvious when someone else thinks of it.

Before Mark wrote, the word *gospel* (good news) meant simply a short announcement of salvation. "The kingdom of God is near," for example, was the "gospel" Jesus preached. St. Paul's "gospel" focused upon Jesus' resurrection because, as Paul saw it, the Reign of God actually began to dawn when Jesus rose.

But St. Mark realized that the whole story about Jesus was "good news"—not the color of his eyes or how tall he was, but the things he said and did, and particularly the way he faced death. So he assembled the teaching and actions of Jesus as he found them recounted in the Church and he arranged them like snapshots in an album, in the form of a simplified story of Jesus' public life. Some commentators describe the result as a synthesis of the theological vision of Paul, who focused upon Jesus' death and resurrection, with the sayings and stories about Jesus' life that characterized the teaching of Peter.

The final product is not a biography. First, the material Mark collected had been circulating orally for more than three decades—in the care not of librarians or scholars but of men concerned for the ongoing life of the Church. And second, Mark makes no attempt at chronological or cause-and-effect order in his presentation. He makes a simplified diagram of Jesus' ministry to dramatize his theme: eight chapters of preaching and healing in Galilee, and then eight more of the fateful journey to Jerusalem and the cross. He inserts incidents into this framework wherever they best illustrate his message, not in the order of actual occurrence.

Going through the finished product, the reader gets a sense of urgency that reflects the time in which Mark was writing. He stood at the end of an era: the Jews who rejected Jesus were on the verge of a suicidal war; the Emperor Nero was murdering Peter and Paul in Rome. Discouragement and false enthusiasms abounded.

And Mark's answer was the cross. Jesus' messiahship is real, and he will return soon to vindicate it. But it can be understood, paradoxically, only in light of the cross. This is the stumbling block for the Jews and their leaders; even Jesus' own disciples failed repeatedly when he tried to make them accept it. And Mark's audience needs to face it too, for only by following their Master on the way to his cross will they enter into his glory.

Matthew

The Gospel of Matthew seems to have been written a generation later (mid-80's) in a Christian synagogue in Syria. It is unknown what connection the work has with the Matthew who was Jesus' disciple, or why it bears the apostle's name. The author may have had access to records that Matthew made; or his community may have claimed Matthew's patronage. In any case, we know that the document we now have was composed in Greek, not translated from Aramaic, and was written after the original Matthew had been dead for some time. It depends upon Mark for most of its narrative, filling this out with teachings of Jesus taken from other sources, the largest of which was used by Luke also.

That its author was a Christian rabbi, from a community that had retained ties with Jewish life as long as possible, is seen from dozens of clues in the writing. For instance, he commonly says "Kingdom of Heaven" instead of "Kingdom of

God," a pious Jewish way of avoiding the casual use of God's name. Style of composition, references to rabbinical customs and disputes, and questions about the continuing validity of the Torah all support the same conclusion. The portrayal of Jesus is heavily Jewish in emphasis, too—he is compared with Moses as the revealer of a new Torah, fulfilling all the aims and promises of the Old Covenant and teaching a more perfect way of life. He is the promised Messiah who will soon return to award the Kingdom to the true Israel that waits for him.

The personality of the author that emerges from the writing is that of a careful teacher, clear and orderly in his thought, willing to repeat or amplify his materials for the sake of presentation. He is less interested in action (he shortens the narratives) and more in explanation (he gives the longest version of many of Jesus' sayings). The result is less dramatic and more solemn than the other evangelists. And where Mark, for example, asks for the willingness to face the cross with Christ, Matthew asks for obedience to all Jesus' commandments—another sign of his Jewish-Christian background.

With all his rabbinical traits, it may seem odd that this author is the most bitter of all against the Pharisees. The explanation lies in the immediate context of his writing. In their preparations for the disastrous war of 66-70 A.D., the Jews had found clear proof that Christians, even Jewish Christians who observed the Law faithfully, could not be trusted to put Judaism first. The Jews were fighting for God's Kingdom, but the Christians knew the Kingdom was not to be obtained that way. So when the remnants of the nation regrouped after their defeat—now under Pharisee leadership, since the Zealots had failed and the Sadducee Temple aristocracy was gone—they formally excommunicated all Christians. But in spite of this hostility, Matthew still preserves an instruction to obey "everything the Pharisees teach" (23:3).

Luke

St. Luke comes from an entirely different world. He is probably the companion mentioned by Paul; an educated Hellenist, perhaps a doctor (Colossians 4:14). The outlook of his writing reflects the breadth of interest and humanity you would expect of such a person.

His Gospel is actually just part one of a two-volume work. After presenting the life of Christianity's founder, he goes on in the Acts of the Apostles to tell how the new faith grew out from Jerusalem "to all Judea and Samaria and even to the ends of the earth" (Acts 1:8). The account ends with St. Paul bringing the gospel to Rome, the capital city, where he "preached the reign of God and taught about the Lord Jesus Christ" (Acts 28:31).

Luke's cultural background appears in his sensitivities—to the nuances of relationship between Jesus and disciple, to the mercy Jesus shows for the poor and suffering, to the tenderness with which Jesus seeks out sinners. More than the other evangelists, he considers stories involving women to be worthy of mention. The same is true of Samaritans, the remnant of the old northern kingdom despised by other Jews. Luke's sensitivities show up also in the way he depicts Jesus' passion—softening some of the violence and horror, bringing out Jesus' nobility and compassion for others.

With Luke we have come a long way from the early community of Jewish Christians in Jerusalem who thought that Jesus' resurrection was the "first fruits" of the general resurrection soon to come. Luke is, in fact, quite explicit that the time of the coming Kingdom is indefinite. He omits the phrase "the Kingdom of God is at hand" where it appears in Matthew and Mark (compare Luke 3:3 with Matthew 3:2, Luke 4:15 with Matthew 4:17, Luke 9:2 with Matthew 10:7, etc.), and he adds it to the teachings of the false messiahs (compare Luke 21:8 with Matthew 24:5).

If Mark presents a gospel of encouragement for the "final" sufferings before the Kingdom's arrival, and Matthew the reinterpretation of Judaism necessary to enter the Kingdom when it comes, Luke has come to terms with the fact that the Church may be around for a good long time before the last day. He emphasizes the Church's task in the world, the daily demands of discipleship, and the peace and joy we can know even now through knowing Jesus and the power of his Holy Spirit.

CHAPTER SEVEN, MATTHEW, MARK, LUKE

Further Readings

1) **Mark's Gospel** — Try reading it straight through at one sitting.
2) **Matthew 23** — Most of the material in this chapter is recorded only by Matthew; it reflects the bitter feelings between his community and official Judaism in the 80's of the first century. But notice how the chapter begins and ends.
3) **Luke 1:1-4** — Luke's statement of purpose. In an educated Greek style, he tells us (1) that he is not an eyewitness, (2) that he is not the first to write down the traditions of the eyewitnesses, (3) that he is working from earlier documents, and (4) that he shares more of our modern concern about the original events than the other evangelists. We have no idea who Theophilus was.

Discussion Starters

1) If the Gospels are not biographies of Jesus, what are they?
2) St. Mark wants us to understand the necessity of the cross as the way to redemption. What is your own attitude toward the cross? Are we to seek out occasions to suffer for the sake of suffering? (Certainly not; but Mark warns us that we are probably avoiding things we should be doing, out of fear of the cross.)
3) Compare Matthew's longer, more solemn version of the Lord's Prayer (6:9-13) with

Luke's shorter one (11:2-4). Which must be closer to the original? Would Luke have left some parts out, or would Matthew have expanded on a shorter prayer? See the same contrast in the two versions of the Beatitudes (Matthew 5:3-12 and Luke 6:20-23). Does it bother you that the evangelists did not have more concern for exact words?

4) "More than any other evangelist, he [Luke] considers stories involving women to be worthy of mention." The New Testament comes from a male-dominated world. What role did women play in the life of Jesus and the early Church? What role should they play in the Church today?

VIII John

If you compare Jesus' teaching as it appears in the first three Gospels with that in the Gospel of John, you will see striking differences in language, in style, even in content.

Jesus' major theme according to Mark, Matthew and Luke is the Reign of God. He proclaims it in the Beatitudes, tells us to pray for its coming, explains it in parable after parable. But in all of John's Gospel the Kingdom is mentioned only in one place (3:3,5). There are no parables. And instead of proclaiming God's Kingdom, Jesus is depicted as speaking in long, circling meditations that return again and again to the same subject — himself. The world without God is lost in darkness, but God has sent Jesus to be man's light and life.

The language shows some relation to Gnosticism, a second- and third-century heresy (from Greek *gnosis* = knowledge; the idea that salvation from this evil world is attained by learning the secret truth about another, more perfect realm. See John 1:18; 3:31; 17:3). Some critics in the past took this to mean that, while the first three Gospels present an essentially *historical* picture of Jesus, the fourth is a *theological* essay written long afterward having only the remotest links with the original disciples of Jesus.

But this late dating of John's Gospel has since been refuted by the discovery of a fragmentary papyrus copy of chapter 18 that dates to the early 100's A.D. Also there are dozens of historical details in John with substantially *more* claim to historical accuracy than their counterparts in the other Gospels. The pool with five porches, for example (5:2), thought by some to be merely symbolic was actually excavated in Jerusalem in our century. So in spite of its differences, modern scholars agree that John's Gospel as we have it is derived from authentic traditions about Jesus and dates no later than 90-95 A.D.

Yet there is no doubt that Mark, Matthew and Luke record Jesus' words more literally. They too had their theologies, as we saw in the previous chapter; and they felt free to modify Jesus' words to some extent. But the fourth Gospel is a translation of Jesus' original message into an entirely new thought-pattern. Instead of the Kingdom of

God, John's Gospel has Jesus speak about "eternal life." Instead of exorcisms vanquishing demons by God's mighty power, John has Jesus perform "signs" which reveal the love and glory of God so that the world may know him. Instead of warning men to prepare for the future judgment of the world on the last day, this Gospel challenges us to decide *now* between the light of truth Jesus brings into the world and the illusions of darkness. Whoever chooses the light has already passed over from death to life, and whoever chooses the darkness over the light is already judged.

This isn't Gnosticism. The Gospel insists that the truth Jesus brings is not just something to know but something to obey: "Love one another as I have loved you." Various Gnostic ideas are explicitly attacked: the material world is not evil, as the Gnostics claimed, but good. It was created by God (1:3) and, though evil now rules it, God still loves it and wills to save it (3:16-17), even to the point of becoming one with it (1:14).

What we have here is a bold attempt to speak to certain patterns of thought prevalent in the Hellenistic world of the first century, patterns which later crystallized into Gnosticism. The heresy of Gnosticism would have done even more damage than it did, had it not been for this kind of missionary effort.

In this context we can raise the question of authorship. Who wrote the fourth Gospel? Was it John, the disciple of Jesus? Not in its finished form. As we have it, it comes from a "school," a community of like-minded people (the "we" of 21:24). There is strong internal evidence that the

71

document went through a series of editings before reaching the final form in which we know it — different styles of Greek, discontinuities in the construction, slight differences of vocabulary. But a school doesn't come into existence without a founder, and this school claims that its founder was "the disciple whom Jesus loved" (21:20).

There is some probability that this "School of John" was first formed in Syria in the 40's among converted Jews who used the kind of theological concepts we have been discussing instead of the strict orthodoxy of the Pharisees. Tradition locates its eventual home in Ephesus, and John's Gospel shows interesting connections with the thought of the Letter to the Ephesians as well as with other New Testament references to Ephesus in Acts 19 and Revelation 2.

Even a hasty reading of John's Gospel gives the sense of a powerful presence behind the words. Many passages seem to reflect liturgical occasions—the great feasts of Passover, Tabernacles, Pentecost, and so on—when the beloved disciple might have addressed the community. Though the final document was repeatedly reworked, we can surmise that he himself stands behind the choice of material and the characteristic emphasis in presenting Jesus.

But whatever the process of its formation, the end product is a unique achievement. The first three Gospels repeat the apocalyptic imagery that Jesus himself used—the approaching end, fire from heaven, and so on—and retain a texture still close to the daily life of rural Palestine. For those who can successfully think themselves back into that world, the Snyoptics offer without question a truer experience of Jesus' actual ministry. But until recent years the necessary historical background wasn't available, and western Christianity has turned, for its deepest insight, to the Gospel of "John the Theologian."

Without using the language of God's Kingdom, John's Gospel presents a powerful invitation to enter it, to share its life. Densely symbolic meditations turn and turn again around the person of Jesus, dizzying us, unhitching us from everyday securities, plunging us into the vision of God's awesome love, and challenging us to dwell in that love. To do this is to know already the glory of risen life that will one day be ours in fullness.

CHAPTER EIGHT, JOHN

Further Readings
1) **John 1:1-18** — The prologue, an ancient liturgical hymn which celebrates the Incarnation of God's Word in Jesus.
2) **John 6** — The Passover sermon. Jesus is the bread that gives eternal life to all who believe.
3) **John 14** — A last supper sermon. Chapters 15-17 repeat the same scene in more expanded form; the end of 14:31 seems originally to have connected with 18:1.

Discussion Starters
1) What is the "eternal life" of which John speaks throughout the Gospel (3:16; 4:14;

5:24; etc.)? Does it connote anything different from the Kingdom of God?

2) "God looked at everything he had made, and found it very good" (Genesis 1:31). Have you ever heard people speak, the way the Gnostics did, as if the material world is evil? In what sense can "the world" really be a principle of evil?

3) John "challenges us to decide *now* between the light of truth Jesus brings into the world and the illusions of darkness." What is this truth that Jesus has brought into the world? What would you consider "illusions of darkness"? See John 3:16-21; 9:4-5.

4) Which has been more meaningful for you personally, the portrait of Jesus in the first three Gospels or that of John?

5) Where does a person get the courage to walk out into the bright light of God's love?

Summing Up:
Three Models of Religion

To the riddle of human existence, the biblical response takes shape gradually, finally achieving its full statement in Jesus of Nazareth. In his life, death and resurrection, he embodies the Kingdom of God, the answer to all human longing. He invites us to embrace and taste that answer now, even as we trust it will one day be established in fullness.

These chapters have traced the history in which this answer emerged. But since a process is best understood when we see its outcome, let us try to summarize the final notion of God's

Kingdom and clarify it by a contrast with other answers that men have believed over the ages. We can do this with the help of three models. They are intended not to exhaust every possible religious attitude, but to provide reference points for our thought—much as the models of "extrovert" and "introvert" help us discuss personality even though few people fit entirely into one type or the other.

First Model: The Closed Cosmos

God —immanent order of the world
World — all that exists
Man — a piece of the world
Evil — whatever threatens world order
Salvation — to fit in and enjoy what's there

The first and most perennial model is based upon the great, turning wheel of nature. Things are born, grow, feed on each other and die—and life goes on. Individual lives emerge for their moment and then recede again into the whole. Ultimate meaning is sought in this endlessly recurring pattern, symbolized by a closed circle or mandala—the wheel of life, the cosmic egg, the carousel.

For a religion of this type the divine is present within every manifestation of the life-force. The great pagan systems of antiquity worshipped the power of bulls, the spell of sex, the sun and stars ruling earth's daily and yearly cycles of sleep and reawakening. The less formulated paganisms of our own time bow to money and youth or military power.

Yet while these things have their significance, they are essentially mundane and finite. They give no hold onto genuinely transcendent reality. In consequence, the man who worships them likewise measures his own being within a closed horizon and finds his definition as a piece of the world. He names good and evil in terms of life's established order; whatever promotes it is good, whatever has the power to disturb it—the alien, the chaotic, or even the merely different— is "unclean" or sinister. (The word *sinister* itself, originally meaning left-handed, embodies the feeling of dread that people used to have at the sight of something out of order in a right-handed world.)

Man's destiny and salvation, in this view, is to be achieved by adjusting to the system, by fitting in, by enjoying life's gifts for their season and then letting go with dignity. A piece of advice written four to five thousand years ago in the *Epic of Gilgamesh* could stand as a classic statement of this first answer to man's riddle:

> Let your belly be full, dance and play day and night
> Let your garments be fresh, your body bathed in water . . .
> Cherish the little one holding your hand
> Let your wife rejoice in your bosom.
> This is the lot of mankind.

But is this all there is? Is our glimpse of infinity just a mirage? To be sure, there are comforts here: the sun rises again after the worst of nights; April showers bring May flowers; we are children of the universe and somehow life goes on. But

79

many would call this a religion for simpler animals, like frogs.

For what about the less gifted who never get their turn—don't they matter? And what about the odd, recurring sense of restlessness, of incompleteness that we still feel even as we ride the crest of life's wave? Why are we awakened to awe and wonder if there is no deeper meaning, nothing to life but a ride on a great carousel? The first religious pattern has no answer for this. In fact, it regards the question as dangerous.

Second Model: Escape

God — opposite of world, "totally other"
World — delusion, unreality
Man — alien, trapped in the world
Evil — worldly desire binding us to world
Salvation — escape

So there arises a second answer to man's riddle, almost the polar opposite of the first — a type of religious formulation in which the life-force is not ultimate meaning and reality but ultimate deception. The reason for our restlessness, the reason for that wordless call that stirs our hearts, is that we don't belong here.

The will-to-life, the *eros* that delights in springtime and health and fights against growing old, is not our true self; it is the impulse of our flesh, the world's lust clamoring to possess us. Our true reality is not this earth-bound, visible body but an invisible soul within, alien and restless in this world because made for another.

This physical world is passing, temporal; our

true home is immaterial and eternal. In this world is darkness, illusion and death; in our true home is light, truth and immortality. The world is the enemy. The god of this second pattern is the antithesis of the world, the "totally other."

To be limited by the horizons of the world, to be deceived by the impulses of the flesh, is to be lost in unreality. But those who can untangle their soul from worldly wants are on the way to salvation. Able finally to face even death untroubled, they will be free to fly to their glorious home above. Hence the disciplines of asceticism and mortification, the cultivation of detachment and stoic indifference. The symbols of this religious type express separation, escape, negation.

While the dimensions of this pattern probably find their fullest realization in the system formulated by the Buddha after his great insight under the Bo tree, they are not unfamiliar to us in the West. Dualistic strains have recurred in Christianity through the centuries.

For many people the only known answers to life's enigma are these two: either pagan ("materialistic") affirmation of such meaning as offered by the world, or the condemnation of worldly existence in favor of some truer ("spiritual") reality. But the Judaeo-Christian tradition actually offers a third and distinct religious answer.

Third Model: The Kingdom of God

God — Creator, transcending world but not remote

World — sacrament of God's glory; not complete

Man — head of creation, Son of God; fully defined in the Risen Christ

Evil — refusal to trust what God is doing

Salvation — God's Kingdom, the future toward which creation strains

Each of the two previous models denies a part of the human reality for the sake of making sense of the rest. The first rules out the impulse toward transcendence; it embraces an established order as if divine, and it labels demonic any challenge to the sovereignty of this order—even the challenge of a prophet who would invite people to something better. The second model refuses to admit the flawed but evident goodness of the world.

The third model, however, holds out both at once. With the religions of escape and negation it recognizes the sad incompleteness of everything finite; but with the religions of worldly life it affirms its roots in the earth. It is not afraid to delight in summer mornings and good wine.

How can it do both? By translating man's restless quest for meaning into expectation, into trust. By discovering that the present situation is only temporary. By projecting a future in which all the promises of creation are fulfilled—in biblical language, the Kingdom of God.

The key word is *future*. Biblical imagery is predominantly of time, not place. The Kingdom of God is not another place, another world, to which our souls might escape at death. Strictly speaking, for this third pattern there is no "other world." The Kingdom is another time, the age to come, the day of resurrection, when our whole being will some-how be reintegrated in a life beyond imagining. And not our being only, but all creation—transformed, aglow with God's presence, making abundantly clear the reason why he made it. The best wine is served at the end.

There is here an acknowledgment of the truth seen by the second model. Biblical religion knows that the present state of the world falls short of its glorious destiny. The Kingdom is not of "this" world or age, but of the "world to come." And yet there is also the truth of the first model. While still in the making, the world is God's handiwork, his self-expression, in which he bodies forth his invisible glory. He transcends it, not as its opposite but as its source and meaning. In the midst of its dreariest and saddest days, we affirm our faith that he rules its history, working somehow unto good.

And God doesn't work alone. The meaning of humanity in this third model is found as the "image and likeness," the visible created counterpart of the invisible God. Though we still belong to the unfinished world, we are also called to participate in authoring it.

Hence the true meaning of that restlessness, that call stirring our hearts: It is the summons not to escape the world, but to love it with God's own love—critical, creative, forgiving, costly. It is the urging of the Spirit to enflesh the Father's glory, to make new the face of the earth.

This is our boast; it can also be our downfall. We can forget that we are only participants in God's work. We can try to grasp at some kind of lordship for ourselves based upon our own shortsighted ideas of what ought to be.

This becomes especially tempting as we learn how fragile our achievements are before the buffetings of history. Is there really a loving purpose behind it all? Instead of joining in the struggle to bring forth the Kingdom, commending the outcome into his hands, we too often shrink back abetted by a religion that says, like the first model, "Don't be a hero; settle for what is." Or like the second, "Forget it; the world has no future anyway."

But either of those answers is too easy. Our nobility and our burden is to go on caring, hoping, laboring at the crossroads of the present and the future, brothers to the frogs and children of God. For even the frogs reflect fragments of glory. And in God's hands, nothing will be lost.